C++ Coding Idea with Example

Billy H. Green

Published by soriful82, 2024.

While every precaution has been taken in the preparation of this book, the publisher assumes no responsibility for errors or omissions, or for damages resulting from the use of the information contained herein.

C++ CODING IDEA WITH EXAMPLE

First edition. September 3, 2024.

ISBN: 979-8227449061

Written by Billy H. Green.

Also by Billy H. Green

C++ Coding Idea with Example

Table of Contents

C++ Coding Idea with Example
Learn C++ Efficiently and Dominate the Programming World

Billy H. Green

Copyright © Billy H. Green

No part of this publication may be reproduced, distributed, or transmitted in any form or by any means, including photocopying, recording, or other electronic or mechanical methods, without the prior written permission of the publisher, except in the case of brief quotations embodied in critical reviews and specific other noncommercial uses permitted by copyright law.

This book is a work of non-fiction. Names, characters, businesses, places, events, locales, and incidents are either the products of the author's experience or used in a factual context. Any resemblance to actual persons, living or dead, or events is coincidental.

The information in this book is provided as is, without warranty of any kind, express or implied, including but not limited to the warranties of merchantability, fitness for a particular purpose, and non-infringement. In no event shall the authors or copyright holders be liable for any claim, damages, or other liability, whether in an action of contract, tort, or otherwise, arising from, out of, or in connection with the book or the use or other dealings in the book.

This book, "C++ Coding Idea: Learn C++ Efficiently and Dominate the Programming World," enhances your understanding of C++ and boost your programming capabilities with practical examples and expert insights.

Introduction

Welcome to C++ Coding Idea with Example: Learn C++ Efficiently and Dominate the Programming World, a comprehensive guide crafted by Billy H. Green to propel you into the forefront of modern programming. This book is not just another programming manual; it is your pathway to mastering C++ through a unique blend of theoretical knowledge and practical application. Have you ever wondered how games like Fortinet or engines like Unreal are built? The answer lies in the power of C++, a language that forms the backbone of numerous software applications and complex systems. With the digital landscape rapidly evolving, proficiency in C++ is desirable and essential. This book demystifies complex concepts and lays a solid foundation, enabling beginners to develop a firm grasp of the language. Dive into the heart of C++ with detailed examples and step-by-step guides that cover everything from basic data types to advanced object-oriented programming techniques. Each chapter is designed to build on the knowledge gained in the previous one, ensuring a structured learning path. What sets this book apart is its focus on real-world applications, providing the context to understand how and why C++ works the way it does.

Imagine creating your software or contributing to significant projects with confidence. By the end of this book, you will learn the syntax of C++ and how to apply it effectively to solve practical programming problems. This book aims to make you proficient in C++ and prepares you to tackle the challenges of the programming world head-on. Start your journey today to become a skilled C++ programmer. Whether developing video games, system software, or high-performance applications, C++ Coding" ng Idea with Example is your gateway to success. Turn the page, and let's embark on this transformative journey together.

What is C++

C++ is a high-level programming language developed by Bjarne Stroustrup as an extension of the C language. It includes object-oriented features, such as classes. Its strong focus on performance and efficiency makes it suitable for applications requiring real-time processing, system programming, and complex computations. C++ supports procedural and object-oriented programming, making it a versatile language for creating large-scale applications, games, system/software development, and even operating systems. It provides rich library support and allows for low-level manipulation of data, which is essential for tasks that require direct control over hardware and memory management.

Getting Started

Here's a simple C++ coding example to help illustrate how to get started with a C++ program:

```cpp
#include <iostream> // Preprocessor directive to include input and output stream
int main() {
std::cout << "Hello, World!"; // Outputs "Hello, World!" to the console
return 0; // Exit status of the program
}
```

This is a live coding example

```
main.cpp                                          Share   Run      Output

1  #include <iostream> // Preprocessor directive to include input and output stream   /tmp/BtKKShxwBV.o
2                                                                                      Hello, World!
3▾ int main() {
4      std::cout << "Hello, World!"; // Outputs "Hello, World!" to the console         === Code Execution Successful ===
5      return 0; // Exit status of the program
6  }
```

Explanation: "Getting started with C++" refers to the initial steps and setup required to begin programming in the C++ language. This involves several key components:

1. **Setting up an Environment**: You'll need an environment where you can write, compile, and run C++ code. This could be a simple text editor and a command-line compiler like GCC, or an integrated development environment (IDE) like Visual Studio or Code::Blocks that offers more features and tools.

2. **Understanding Basic Syntax**: As demonstrated in the example, understanding C++ syntax is crucial. This includes knowing how to write functions, manage input/output, and utilize libraries like <iostream> for basic operations.

3. **Compiling and Running**: After writing the code, it must be compiled into an executable file. This is done using a C++ compiler which translates the C++ code into machine code that the computer can execute. Running the compiled program will perform the tasks coded in it, such as printing "Hello, World!" to the console in the example.

4. **Learning Standard Library**: C++ has a powerful standard library that includes functions for handling files, strings, and complex data structures among others. Getting acquainted with this library is essential for effective C++ programming.

5. **Practicing Basic Concepts**: Start with basic concepts such as variables, data types, control structures (if-else, loops), functions, and gradually move to more complex topics like object-oriented programming, templates, and error handling.

By going through these steps, you can begin to write simple programs in C++ and gradually build up to more complex applications.

Syntax

Here's a simple example of C++ syntax:

This is Code


```cpp
#include <iostream> // Preprocessor directive to include input-output stream
int main() { // Main function where the execution begins
std::cout << "Hello, World!"; // Statement to output text to the console
return 0; // Return statement indicating successful execution
}
```

This is a live coding example

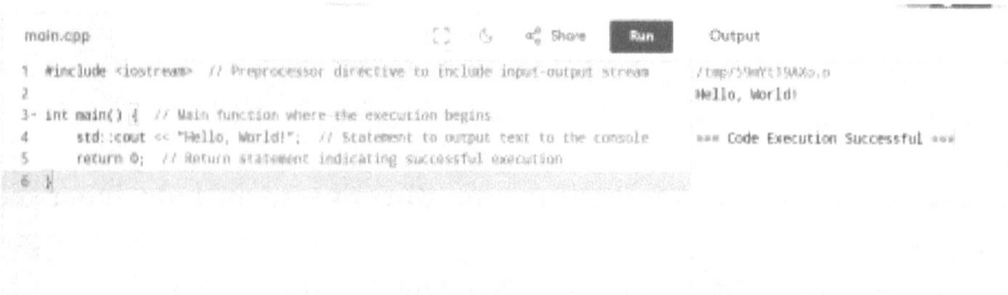

```cpp
main.cpp                                    Share    Run        Output

1  #include <iostream>  // Preprocessor directive to include input-output stream    /tmp/59mYt19AXo.o
2                                                                                    Hello, World!
3- int main() {  // Main function where the execution begins
4      std::cout << "Hello, World!";  // Statement to output text to the console     *** Code Execution Successful ***
5      return 0;  // Return statement indicating successful execution
6  }
```


```cpp
main.cpp                                    Share    Run        Output

1  #include <iostream>  // Preprocessor directive to include input-output stream    /tmp/59mYt19AXo.o
2                                                                                    Hello, World!
3- int main() {  // Main function where the execution begins
4      std::cout << "Hello, World!";  // Statement to output text to the console     *** Code Execution Successful ***
5      return 0;  // Return statement indicating successful execution
6  }
```

C++ CODING IDEA WITH EXAMPLE

Explanation of C++ Syntax: C++ syntax refers to the set of rules that define how the code must be written for the compiler to understand and execute it. This includes how to declare variables, define functions, use operators, and structure your program. Here's a breakdown of the elements in the example:

- **Preprocessor Directive**: #include <iostream> is a preprocessor directive that tells the compiler to include the Standard Input Output stream library before actual compilation begins, enabling use of std::cout.
- **Main Function**: int main() is the main function where every C++ program begins execution. The function must return an integer, with 0 typically signaling successful execution.
- **Statements**: Inside the main function, std::cout << "Hello, World!"; is a statement that outputs text to the console. In C++, every statement ends with a semicolon (;).
- **Return Statement**: return 0; terminates the main function and returns the value 0 to the calling process (usually the operating system), indicating that the program ended successfully.

The syntax of C++ is crucial for structuring the code correctly and ensuring that it compiles and runs as expected. It involves the correct use of braces for defining scopes, semicolons to end statements, and correct grammar rules for composing various program elements.

Statements

Here's a simple example of C++ statements:

This is Code


```cpp
#include <iostream>
int main() {
int x = 5; // Statement 1
x = x + 2; // Statement 2
std::cout << x; // Statement 3
return 0; // Statement 4
}
```

This is a live coding example

```cpp
main.cpp                                    Share    Run        Output

1   #include <iostream>                               /tmp/c2F4eEmj8r.o
2                                                      7
3·  int main() {
4       int x = 5;        // Statement 1              === Code Execution Successful ===
5       x = x + 2;        // Statement 2
6       std::cout << x;   // Statement 3
7       return 0;         // Statement 4
8   }
```

Explanation: In C++, statements are the basic building blocks of a program that instruct the computer to perform a specific task. Each statement ends with a semicolon (;), which marks the end of the logical instruction or action.

- **Statement 1** (int x = 5;) declares an integer variable x and initializes it with the value 5.
- **Statement 2** (x = x + 2;) modifies the value of x by adding 2 to it.
- **Statement 3** (std::cout << x;) uses the output stream cout to print the value of x to the console.
- **Statement 4** (return 0;) ends the main function and returns 0 to the operating system, indicating that the program has executed successfully.

Each of these statements performs a distinct operation, and together they create a simple program that updates a variable and outputs the result. This demonstrates how C++ statements control the flow and behavior of the program.

Output (Print Text)

Here's an example of how to output (print) text in C++:

This is Code


```cpp
#include <iostream>
int main() {
std::cout << "Hello, world!" << std::endl;
return 0;
}
```

This is a live coding example

```
main.cpp                              Share    Run       Output

1  #include <iostream>                          /tmp/re88B1AWbO.o
2                                               Hello, world!
3▾ int main() {
4      std::cout << "Hello, world!" << std::endl;
5      return 0;                                === Code Execution Successful ===
6  }
```

C++ CODING IDEA WITH EXAMPLE

Explanation: In C++, the std::cout object is used to send output to the standard output stream, usually the screen. This object is part of the iostream library, which handles input and output in C++. The << operator is used with std::cout to send data to the output.

- std::cout << "Hello, world!" prints the text "Hello, world!" to the standard output.
- std::endl is a manipulator that inserts a newline character into the output stream and flushes the stream, ensuring that all output is immediately displayed. Alternatively, you can use '\n' for a newline without flushing the stream.

This basic mechanism is how you display messages to the user, debug information, or any other textual data you need to output from a C++ program.

New Lines

Here's a coding example in C++ that demonstrates the use of new lines:

This is Code


```cpp
#include <iostream>

int main() {
std::cout << "Hello, World!\n";
std::cout << "This is the second line.\n";
return 0;
}
```

This is a live coding example

```
main.cpp                          [] ⌂  ⌁ Share   Run        Output

1  #include <iostream>                               /tmp/J6PMb19sWE.o
2                                                    Hello, World!
3▾ int main() {                                      This is the second line.
4     std::cout << "Hello, World!\n";
5     std::cout << "This is the second line.\n";
6     return 0;                                      === Code Execution Successful ===
7  }
```

Explanation: In C++, new lines can be introduced in several ways. The most common method is by using the newline character \n, which is included within string literals in the code above. This character tells the output stream to move the cursor to the start of the next line of the output console, effectively creating a new line.

When std::cout encounters \n, it outputs all the previous characters up to the newline character and then moves to the next line. This is useful for formatting output to make it more readable or to adhere to certain output formats.

Additionally, C++ streams like std::cout can handle new lines using manipulators like std::endl, which outputs a newline character and flushes the output buffer. This is slightly different from \n because it also ensures that all output is written to the target device immediately.

Comments

Here's a coding example that demonstrates the use of comments in C++:

This is Code


```cpp
#include <iostream>
int main() {
// This is a single-line comment
std::cout << "Hello, World!" << std::endl; // This prints "Hello, World!" to the console
/*
This is a multi-line comment.
It can span multiple lines.
Comments like this are useful for longer explanations.
*/
int a = 5; // Initialize variable 'a' with the value 5
return 0; // End of the main function
}
```

This is a live coding example

Explanation of C++ Comments

In C++, comments are used to annotate the code and provide explanations or notes that are not executed by the compiler. They help make the code more understandable to humans, whether for the original programmer or others reading the code.

Single-Line Comment:

Syntax: // comment text

Everything following // on that line is considered a comment and will be ignored by the compiler.

Example: // This is a single-line comment

Multi-Line Comment:

Syntax: /* comment text */

Anything between /* and */ is treated as a comment, and it can span multiple lines.

Example:

```
/*

This is a multi-line comment.

It can span multiple lines.

*/
```

Comments are crucial for explaining what the code is doing, why certain decisions were made, or to temporarily disable parts of the code during debugging. They don't affect the program's execution but significantly contribute to code readability and maintainability.

Variables

Here's an example of defining variables in C++:

Code.


```cpp
#include <iostream>
using namespace std;
int main() {
int age = 30;
double salary = 85000.50;
char grade = 'A';
cout << "Age: " << age << ", Salary: " << salary << ", Grade: " << grade << endl;
return 0;
}
```

This is a live coding example

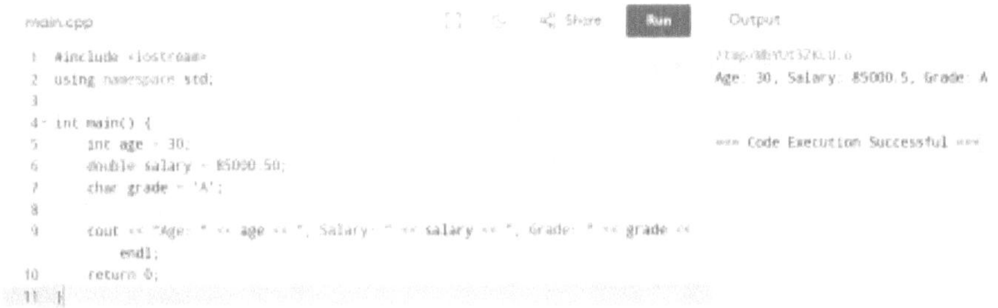

Explanation:

In C++, a variable is a storage location in the computer's memory having a specific type that determines the size and layout of the memory; the range of values that can be stored within that memory; and the set of operations that can be applied to the variable.

- **int age = 30;** - This line declares a variable named age of type int (integer), used for whole numbers, and initializes it to 30.
- **double salary = 85000.50;** - This declares a variable salary of type double, which is a floating-point type used for numbers with decimals. It's initialized to 85000.50.
- **char grade = 'A';** - This declares a char (character) variable grade, initialized to 'A'.

Each variable in C++ must be declared with a specific type which dictates what kind of values it can hold. Variables are fundamental in C++ as they are used to store information needed by the program. They can be assigned values and changed throughout the program, acting as containers for storing data in memory.

Declare Multiple Variables

Here's an example of declaring multiple variables in C++:

This is Code


```cpp
#include <iostream>
    int main() {
    int a = 5, b = 10;
    char c = 'z';
    double d = 3.14, e = 2.718;
    return 0;
}
```

This is a live coding example

Explanation

In C++, you can declare multiple variables of the same type in a single statement by separating them with commas. In the example above, two integer variables a and b are declared and initialized in the same line. Similarly, two double variables d and e are declared and initialized together.

It's also possible to declare multiple variables of different types in separate statements within the same block of code. Here, char c is declared separately from the integers and doubles. This approach helps in keeping the code clean and organized, allowing for better type management and reducing the chances of errors related to variable types. Each variable can also be initialized during its declaration, as shown, which is a common practice for setting initial values.

Identifiers

Here's a coding example that includes C++ identifiers:

Live Code


```cpp
#include <iostream>
int main() {
int age = 25;
double salary = 45000.50;
char grade = 'A';
std::cout << "Age: " << age << ", Salary: " << salary << ", Grade: " << grade << std::endl;
return 0;
}
```

This is a live coding example

```cpp
main.cpp                                    Share    Run     Output

 1   #include <iostream>                          /tmp/CPPX3STpab.o
 2                                                 Age: 25, Salary: 45000.5, Grade: A
 3 - int main() {
 4       int age = 25;
 5       double salary = 45000.50;               === Code Execution Successful ===
 6       char grade = 'A';
 7
 8       std::cout << "Age: " << age << ", Salary: " << salary << ", Grade: " << grade
             << std::endl;
 9       return 0;
10   }
```

Explanation of C++ Identifiers: In C++, identifiers are the names given to entities such as variables, functions, classes, and objects that are used to identify them uniquely within the scope where they are declared. In the example above, age, salary, and grade are identifiers associated with different variables. Similarly, main is an identifier used for the function name.

Identifiers in C++ must begin with a letter (uppercase or lowercase) or an underscore (_), followed by letters, digits, or underscores. They are case-sensitive, so age, Age, and AGE would be considered different identifiers. Proper naming of identifiers makes the code more readable and maintainable, as it can describe the purpose or type of the data they represent.

Constants

Here's an example of using constants in C++:

This is Live Code


```cpp
#include <iostream>
using namespace std;
int main() {
const int LIGHT_SPEED = 299792; // Declaring a constant
cout << "The speed of light is " << LIGHT_SPEED << " kilometers per second." << endl;
return 0;
}
```

This is a live coding example

```
main.cpp                                    Share    Run         Output

1   #include <iostream>                                  c++ prog/lib/383/main.o
2   using namespace std;                                 The speed of light is 299792 kilometers per second.
3
4   int main() {
5       const int LIGHT_SPEED = 299792;  // Declaring a constant    *** Code Execution Successful ***
6       cout << "The speed of light is " << LIGHT_SPEED << " kilometers per second."
            << endl;
7       return 0;
8   }
```

Explanation: In C++, constants are fixed values that the program may not alter during its execution. These can be declared using the const keyword followed by the data type, and then the name and value. Once a constant is set, its value cannot be changed.

Constants are useful for giving descriptive names to values that appear in various places in your code. This can make your program easier to read and maintain. For example, in the code above, LIGHT_SPEED is used to represent the speed of light in kilometers per second. By using a constant, you ensure that this value is consistent wherever it's used in your program and can easily update it in one place if necessary.

User Input

Here's a simple example of how to handle user input in C++:

Live Code


```cpp
#include <iostream>
using namespace std;
int main() {
int number;
cout << "Enter an integer: ";
cin >> number;
cout << "You entered: " << number << endl;
return 0;
}
```

This is a live coding example

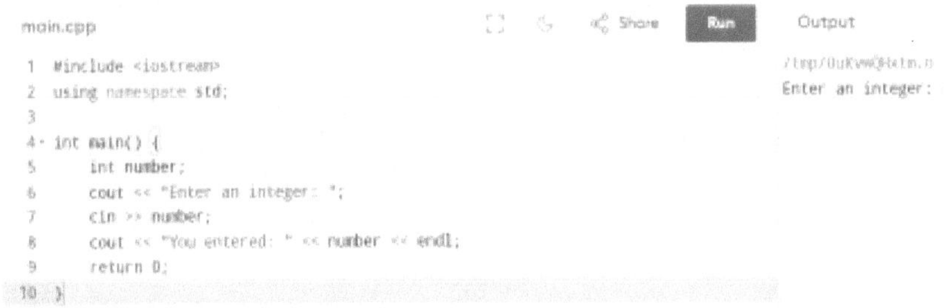

```
main.cpp                            Share   Run      Output

1  #include <iostream>                        /tmp/UuKvw@4xtn.n
2  using namespace std;                       Enter an integer:
3
4  int main() {
5      int number;
6      cout << "Enter an integer: ";
7      cin >> number;
8      cout << "You entered: " << number << endl;
9      return 0;
10 }
```

Explanation: In C++, user input can be taken from the console using the cin object, which is part of the iostream library. The example above starts by including the iostream header file that contains definitions of the cin and cout objects used for input and output operations, respectively.

- **cin**: This object represents the standard input stream. It is used with the extraction operator (>>), which reads data from the input stream.
- **int number;**: This line declares an integer variable named number.
- **cin >> number;**: This line waits for the user to enter an integer, which cin reads from the keyboard input and stores in the variable number.
- **cout << "You entered: " << number << endl;**: This line outputs the text "You entered: " followed by the value of number, ending with a newline.

This basic input mechanism can be extended to read different data types and multiple values, making it a fundamental aspect of interactive C++ programs.

Data Types

Here's an example of C++ data types in a simple program:

Live Code


```cpp
#include <iostream>
using namespace std;
int main() {
int anInteger = 42;
double aDouble = 3.14159;
char aCharacter = 'A';
bool aBoolean = true;
cout << "Integer: " << anInteger << endl;
cout << "Double: " << aDouble << endl;
cout << "Character: " << aCharacter << endl;
cout << "Boolean: " << aBoolean << endl;
return 0;
}
```

This is a live coding example

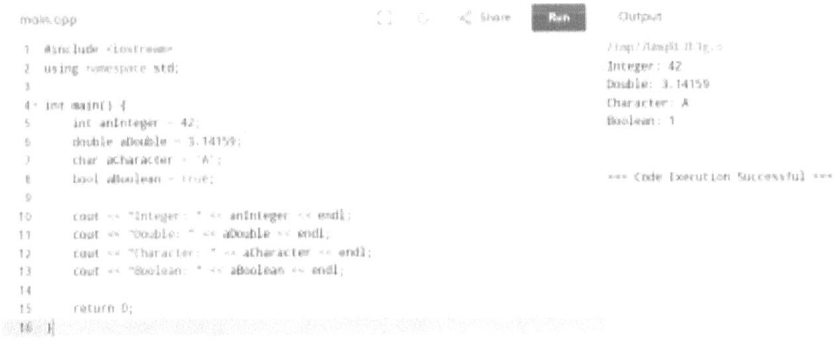

Explanation of C++ Data Types: C++ provides a rich set of built-in as well as user-defined data types. Here are the basic categories:

1. **Primitive Data Types**: These include integers (int), floating-point numbers (float, double), characters (char), and boolean values (bool). These data types are built into the language and provide the foundation for building other data types.
2. **Derived Data Types**: These are formed from the primitive data types and include arrays, pointers, and references. For example, you can have an array of integers or a pointer to a double.
3. **User-Defined Data Types**: C++ allows users to define their own types using structures (struct), unions, and classes (class). These types can encapsulate data and functions that operate on the data, providing a way to model more complex entities.
4. **Enumerated Data Type**: Defined using the enum keyword, this type consists of a set of named integer constants to make a program easier to read and maintain.

Each data type in C++ is designed to optimize storage and improve the performance of various operations on the data. The choice of data type depends on the specific needs of the application, such as the precision of calculations or the memory usage requirements.

Numeric Data Types

Here's a coding example demonstrating C++ numeric data types:

This is Live Code


```cpp
#include <iostream>
using namespace std;
int main() {
int integer = 5; // Integer
double floatingPoint = 5.99; // Floating-point number
char character = 'A'; // Character type (numeric representation of ASCII values)
bool boolean = true; // Boolean (True or False, represented as 1 or 0)
cout << "Integer: " << integer << endl;
cout << "Floating Point: " << floatingPoint << endl;
cout << "Character (as number): " << static_cast<int>(character) << endl;
cout << "Boolean (as number): " << boolean << endl;
return 0;
}
```

This is a live coding example

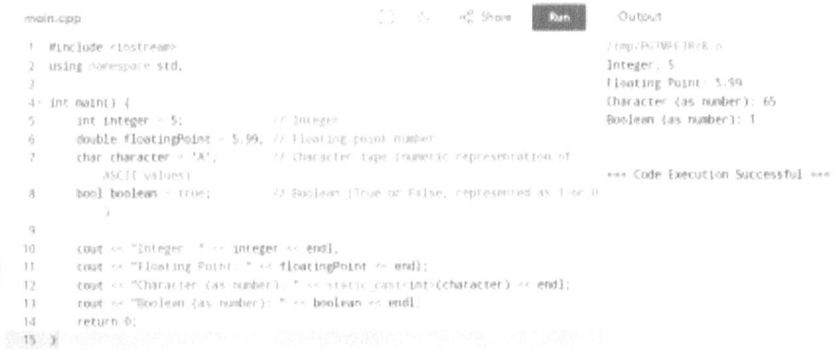

Explanation: C++ offers several numeric data types that allow programmers to select the appropriate type according to the needs of the application, balancing between memory usage and precision.

1. **Integer Types (int, short, long, long long)** - These are used to store whole numbers. They can be either signed (can hold both positive and negative values) or unsigned (only positive values).
2. **Floating Point Types (float, double, long double)** - These are used for storing numbers with fractional parts. The choice between float, double, and long double depends on the precision required and the amount of memory available.
3. **Character Type (char)** - Technically a numeric type because it stores integers that represent character codes (like ASCII values). It's often used to hold characters in coding.
4. **Boolean Type (bool)** - It represents truth values (true and false). In a numeric context, true is typically represented as 1, and false as 0.

Each type consumes a different amount of memory and has its own range of values it can represent, affecting both the performance and accuracy of the applications they are used in.

Boolean Data Types

Here's a coding example using the C++ Boolean data type:

This is Live Code


```cpp
#include <iostream>
using namespace std;
int main() {
bool isSunny = true;
cout << "Is it sunny? " << isSunny << endl; // Outputs: Is it sunny? 1
isSunny = false;
cout << "Is it sunny now? " << isSunny << endl; // Outputs: Is it sunny now? 0
return 0;
}
```

This is a live coding example

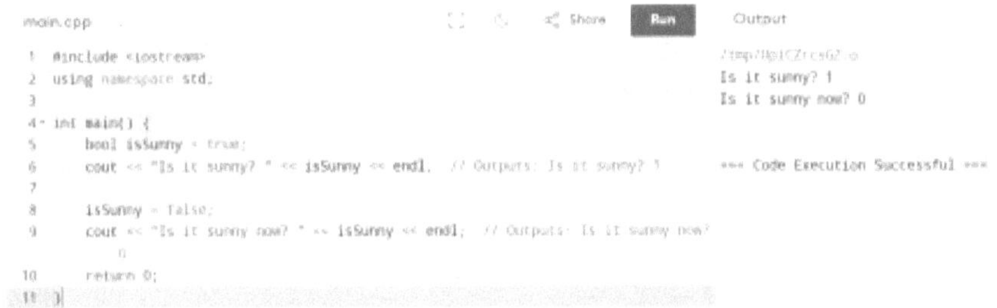

main.cpp — Share — Run — Output

```cpp
1  #include <iostream>
2  using namespace std;
3
4  int main() {
5      bool isSunny = true;
6      cout << "Is it sunny? " << isSunny << endl;   // Outputs: Is it sunny? 1
7
8      isSunny = false;
9      cout << "Is it sunny now? " << isSunny << endl;   // Outputs: Is it sunny now?
           0
10     return 0;
11 }
```

/tmp/ Up1CZrcsG2.o
Is it sunny? 1
Is it sunny now? 0

*** Code Execution Successful ***

Explanation: In C++, the Boolean data type is represented by the keyword bool. It can hold one of two values: true or false. When a Boolean is outputted, true is typically represented as 1 and false as 0. This data type is particularly useful in controlling flow with conditions and decisions in programming. It's fundamental for operations that involve logic, such as comparisons and conditions that determine which code segment should be executed next.

Character Data Types

Here's an example of using C++ character data types in code:

This is Code


```cpp
#include <iostream>
    using namespace std;
    int main() {
    char letter = 'A';
    unsigned char uLetter = 'B';
    signed char sLetter = 'C';
    cout << "Character: " << letter << endl;
    cout << "Unsigned Character: " << uLetter << endl;
    cout << "Signed Character: " << sLetter << endl;
    return 0;
    }
```

This is a live coding example

```cpp
main.cpp                                    Share   Run        Output

1   #include <iostream>                                 /tmp/R3Kkx93jCL.o
2   using namespace std;                                Character: A
3                                                       Unsigned Character: B
4 - int main() {                                        Signed Character: C
5       char letter = 'A';
6       unsigned char uLetter = 'B';
7       signed char sLetter = 'C';                      === Code Execution Successful ===
8
9       cout << "Character: " << letter << endl;
10      cout << "Unsigned Character: " << uLetter << endl;
11      cout << "Signed Character: " << sLetter << endl;
12
13      return 0;
14  }
```

Explanation of C++ Character Data Types:

In C++, character data types are used to store characters and are typically represented by the char keyword. Each character occupies one byte of memory, and the data type can represent a character from a character set (like ASCII or Unicode depending on the system).

- **char**: This is the basic character data type. It can be signed or unsigned based on the compiler, but typically it represents signed values. This means it can hold ASCII values from -128 to 127.
- **unsigned char**: This represents a character using unsigned numbers, so it can store values from 0 to 255. This is useful when you want to work with the full range of 8-bit data without negative values, often used in scenarios involving binary data and byte-specific manipulations.
- **signed char**: Explicitly defines a character as signed, ensuring that it can hold negative values (from -128 to 127). This specification is important when the character data will be used in mathematical computations that might involve negative numbers.

Using these types, C++ allows for efficient manipulation of character data and direct access to modifying and interacting with binary data in a straightforward manner.

String Data Types

Here's a coding example using C++ string data types:

This is live Code


```cpp
#include <iostream>
#include <string>
int main() {
std::string greeting = "Hello, World!";
std::cout << greeting << std::endl;
return 0;
}
```

This is a live coding example

```
main.cpp                              Share   Run        Output

1  #include <iostream>                           /tmp/a0c91w6PZs.o
2  #include <string>                             Hello, World!
3
4* int main() {
5      std::string greeting = "Hello, World!";   === Code Execution Successful ===
6      std::cout << greeting << std::endl;
7      return 0;
8  }
```

Explanation:

In C++, the std::string is a data type provided by the C++ Standard Library to represent sequences of characters and manage strings of text. Unlike the C-style character arrays that require manual management of memory and other low-level operations, std::string handles these operations automatically.

- **Dynamic Size**: Unlike arrays, std::string can change its size dynamically to accommodate the length of the text it holds.
- **Member Functions**: It comes with a number of useful member functions for string manipulation, such as append(), insert(), find(), and replace().
- **Safety**: std::string provides more safety by managing memory automatically and reducing the risk of buffer overflow, which is common with C-style character arrays.
- **Convenience**: It supports operations like concatenation using + operator and comparison using relational operators like ==, !=, <, etc.

Using std::string is recommended for handling text in C++ due to its ease of use and robust set of features designed to work with strings efficiently and safely.

Operators

Here's an example of using C++ operators:

This is Live Code


```cpp
#include <iostream>
using namespace std;
int main() {
int a = 5;
int b = 3;
int sum = a + b; // Using the addition operator
int product = a * b; // Using the multiplication operator
bool isEqual = (a == b); // Using the equality operator
cout << "Sum: " << sum << endl;
cout << "Product: " << product << endl;
cout << "Are a and b equal? " << isEqual << endl;
return 0;
}
```

This is a live coding example

```cpp
main.cpp                                    Share   Run        Output

 1   #include <iostream>                              /tmp/3QQF8RIvE0.o
 2   using namespace std;                             Sum: 8
 3                                                    Product: 15
 4 ▾ int main() {                                     Are a and b equal? 0
 5       int a = 5;
 6       int b = 3;
 7       int sum = a + b;  // Using the addition operator    *** Code Execution Successful ***
 8       int product = a * b;  // Using the multiplication operator
 9       bool isEqual = (a == b);  // Using the equality operator
10
11       cout << "Sum: " << sum << endl;
12       cout << "Product: " << product << endl;
13       cout << "Are a and b equal? " << isEqual << endl;
14
15       return 0;
16   }
```

Explanation: C++ operators are symbols that perform operations on variables and values. They are used to execute arithmetic, comparison, logical, bitwise, assignment, and other types of operations. Here are some types of operators in C++:

- **Arithmetic Operators**: +, -, *, /, and % are used for basic mathematical calculations.
- **Comparison Operators**: ==, !=, >, <, >=, and <= are used to compare two values. These operators return a Boolean value (true or false).
- **Logical Operators**: && (logical AND), || (logical OR), and ! (logical NOT) are used to combine Boolean expressions.
- **Assignment Operators**: =, +=, -= etc., are used to assign values to variables.
- **Bitwise Operators**: &, |, ^, ~, <<, >> operate at the bit level, which is useful for tasks involving low-level manipulations.
- **Other Operators**: C++ also includes other specialized operators like the address (&) and dereference (*) operators for pointers, and the scope resolution operator (::).

Operators are fundamental to programming in C++, as they allow the manipulation of data and control the logic flow of the program.

Page |

Assignment Operators

Here's a coding example using C++ assignment operators:

This is Live Code


```cpp
#include <iostream>
    int main() {
    int a = 5; // Basic assignment
    int b;
    b = a; // Direct assignment
    b += 2; // Addition assignment
    b *= 3; // Multiplication assignment
    std::cout << "The value of b is: " << b << std::endl; // Output will be 21
    return 0;
    }
```

This is a live coding example

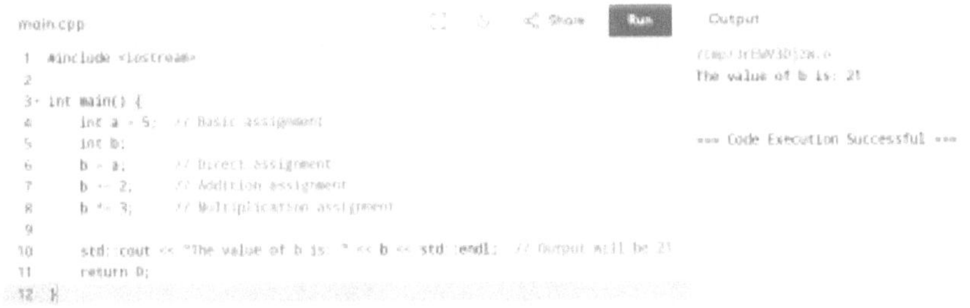

Explanation:

C++ assignment operators are used to assign values to variables. The most basic assignment operator is =, which simply assigns the value on its right to the variable on its left.

- **Direct Assignment** (=): This operator assigns the right-hand side expression to the left-hand side variable. For example, b = a; assigns the value of a to b.
- **Compound Assignment**: These operators modify the variable and assign it a new value in a single step. Common compound assignment operators include:
    - +=: Adds the right operand to the left operand and assigns the result to the left operand. Example: b += 2; is equivalent to b = b + 2;.
    - *=: Multiplies the right operand with the left operand and assigns the result to the left operand. Example: b *= 3; is equivalent to b = b * 3;.

Other compound assignment operators include -= (subtraction assignment), /= (division assignment), and %= (modulus assignment), among others. These operators provide a shorthand way to update the value of a variable based on its current value and the result of an arithmetic operation.

Comparison Operators

Here's a coding example using C++ comparison operators:

This is Live Code


```cpp
#include <iostream>
using namespace std;
int main() {
int a = 5;
int b = 10;
// Using comparison operators
cout << "a == b: " << (a == b) << endl; // Equal to
cout << "a != b: " << (a != b) << endl; // Not equal to
cout << "a < b: " << (a < b) << endl; // Less than
cout << "a > b: " << (a > b) << endl; // Greater than
cout << "a <= b: " << (a <= b) << endl; // Less than or equal to
cout << "a >= b: " << (a >= b) << endl; // Greater than or equal to
return 0;
}
```

This is a live coding example

```cpp
main.cpp                                    Share   Run      Output

 1   #include <iostream>                              /tmp/1RfScBbxE.o
 2   using namespace std;                             a == b: 0
 3                                                    a != b: 1
 4 - int main() {                                     a < b: 1
 5       int a = 5;                                   a > b: 0
 6       int b = 10;                                  a <= b: 1
 7                                                    a >= b: 0
 8       // Using comparison operators
 9       cout << "a == b: " << (a == b) << endl;    // Equal to
10       cout << "a != b: " << (a != b) << endl;    // Not equal to      *** Code Execution Successful ***
11       cout << "a < b: " << (a < b) << endl;      // Less than
12       cout << "a > b: " << (a > b) << endl;      // Greater than
13       cout << "a <= b: " << (a <= b) << endl;    // Less than or equal to
14       cout << "a >= b: " << (a >= b) << endl;    // Greater than or equal to
15       return 0;
16   }
```

Explanation: C++ comparison operators are used to compare two values or expressions and return a boolean value based on the validity of the comparison. Here's what each operator does:

- ==: Checks if the values of two operands are equal. If yes, it returns true.
- !=: Checks if the values of two operands are not equal. If yes, it returns true.
- <: Checks if the value of the left operand is less than the value of the right operand. If yes, it returns true.
- >: Checks if the value of the left operand is greater than the value of the right operand. If yes, it returns true.
- <=: Checks if the value of the left operand is less than or equal to the value of the right operand. If yes, it returns true.
- >=: Checks if the value of the left operand is greater than or equal to the value of the right operand. If yes, it returns true.

These operators are fundamental in making decisions and controlling the flow of programs by allowing conditional testing of values.

Page |

Logical Operators

Here's an example of using C++ logical operators:

This is Live Code


```cpp
#include <iostream>
using namespace std;
int main() {
bool a = true;
bool b = false;
cout << "a && b: " << (a && b) << endl; // Logical AND
cout << "a || b: " << (a || b) << endl; // Logical OR
cout << "!a: " << (!a) << endl; // Logical NOT
return 0;
}
```

This is a live coding example

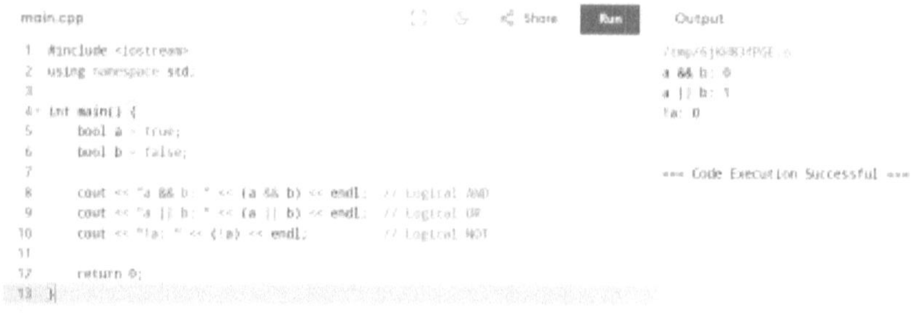

```
main.cpp                                    Share    Run      Output

 1  #include <iostream>                              /tmp/6j6983tPGE.o
 2  using namespace std.                             a && b: 0
 3                                                   a || b: 1
 4  int main() {                                     !a: 0
 5      bool a = true;
 6      bool b = false;
 7                                                   === Code Execution Successful ===
 8      cout << "a && b: " << (a && b) << endl;  // Logical AND
 9      cout << "a || b: " << (a || b) << endl;  // Logical OR
10      cout << "!a: " << (!a) << endl;          // Logical NOT
11
12      return 0;
13  }
```

Explanation: C++ logical operators are used to form compound conditions by combining two or more conditions. They are primarily used in control flow statements like if, while, and for loops. The three main logical operators are:

- **Logical AND (&&):** Returns true if both operands are true. In the example, a && b returns false because b is false.
- **Logical OR (||):** Returns true if at least one of the operands is true. In the example, a || b returns true because a is true.
- **Logical NOT (!):** Inverts the boolean value of its operand. If the operand is true, it returns false, and vice versa. In the example, !a returns false because a is true.

These operators are fundamental for creating complex logical expressions that control the flow of execution in programs based on various conditions.

Strings

Here's an example of using C++ strings:

This is Live Code


```cpp
#include <iostream>
#include <string> // Include the string library
int main() {
std::string greeting = "Hello, World!";
std::cout << greeting << std::endl;
return 0;
}
```

This is a live coding example

```
main.cpp                          [] 〔 ⤳ Share  Run    Output

1  #include <iostream>                          /tmp/0p5999rWlS.o
2  #include <string> // Include the string library   Hello, World!
3
4▾ int main() {
5      std::string greeting = "Hello, World!";        === Code Execution Successful ===
6      std::cout << greeting << std::endl;
7      return 0;
8  }
```

Explanation: In C++, strings are used to store and manipulate text. The std::string class, which is part of the C++ Standard Library, provides a rich set of methods and operators to work with strings, making it a powerful and flexible alternative to the C-style strings (arrays of characters).

The std::string class in C++ automatically manages memory, grows dynamically as needed, and provides safety features that are not available with C-style strings. It supports common operations like concatenation, comparison, and assignment directly with overloaded operators, making the code more intuitive and less prone to errors like buffer overflows. The example above includes the string library, creates a string variable called greeting with the value "Hello, World!", and outputs it to the console. This demonstrates the ease with which text data can be handled in C++.

String Concatenation

Here's an example of C++ string concatenation:

This is Live Code


```cpp
#include <iostream>
#include <string>
int main() {
std::string first = "Hello";
std::string second = " World!";
std::string combined = first + second;
std::cout << combined; // Outputs: Hello World!
return 0;
}
```

- **This is a live coding example**

```
main.cpp                                    Share    Run        Output
 1  #include <iostream>                                      /tmp/fUVQ2znzyD.o
 2  #include <string>                                        Hello World!
 3
 4  int main() {                                             === Code Execution Successful ===
 5      std::string first = "Hello";
 6      std::string second = " World!";
 7      std::string combined = first + second;
 8      std::cout << combined;   // Outputs: Hello World!
 9      return 0;
10  }
```

Explanation: In C++, string concatenation refers to the process of appending one string to the end of another string. This can be achieved using the + operator when dealing with std::string objects. The result is a new string that is the combination of the two operand strings.

The std::string class in C++ handles the memory management automatically, which makes string manipulation more intuitive compared to using C-style strings (char arrays). When two std::string objects are concatenated, a new string is created that includes the characters from both source strings in the order they were concatenated. This method is efficient for regular use in applications where string manipulation is necessary.

Numbers and Strings

Here's an example of using numbers and strings in C++:

This is Live Code


```cpp
#include <iostream>
#include <string>
int main() {
int number = 5; // A number
double decimal = 3.14; // A decimal number
std::string text = "Hello"; // A string
std::cout << "Number: " << number << std::endl;
std::cout << "Decimal: " << decimal << std::endl;
std::cout << "String: " << text << std::endl;
return 0;
}
```

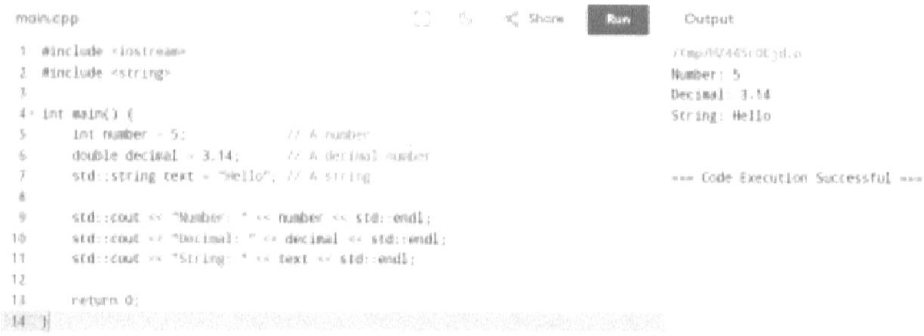

```cpp
main.cpp                                    Share    Run        Output

1  #include <iostream>                             /tmp/HZ445rdtjd.o
2  #include <string>                               Number: 5
3                                                  Decimal: 3.14
4  int main() {                                    String: Hello
5      int number = 5;            // A number
6      double decimal = 3.14;     // A decimal number
7      std::string text = "Hello", // A string     === Code Execution Successful ===
8
9      std::cout << "Number: " << number << std::endl;
10     std::cout << "Decimal: " << decimal << std::endl;
11     std::cout << "String: " << text << std::endl;
12
13     return 0;
14  }
```

This is a live coding example

Explanation:

In C++, **numbers** can be represented using various data types such as int for integers, double for floating-point numbers, and others like float and long. These types allow you to work with numerical data, perform mathematical operations, and manipulate values in various ways.

Strings, on the other hand, are sequences of characters used to store text. In C++, strings can be handled using the std::string class, which is part of the C++ Standard Library. This class provides a rich set of functions and methods for string manipulation, including appending, comparing, searching, and modifying strings.

This code snippet demonstrates how to declare and initialize numbers and a string, and how to output them using std::cout. The use of different data types allows for a variety of operations and applications in C++ programming.

String Length

Here's an example demonstrating how to find the length of a string in C++:

This is Live Code

```cpp
#include <iostream>
#include <string> // Include the string library to use the string class
int main() {
std::string myString = "Hello, world!";
std::cout << "The length of the string is: " << myString.length() << std::endl;
return 0;
}
```

- **This is a live coding example**

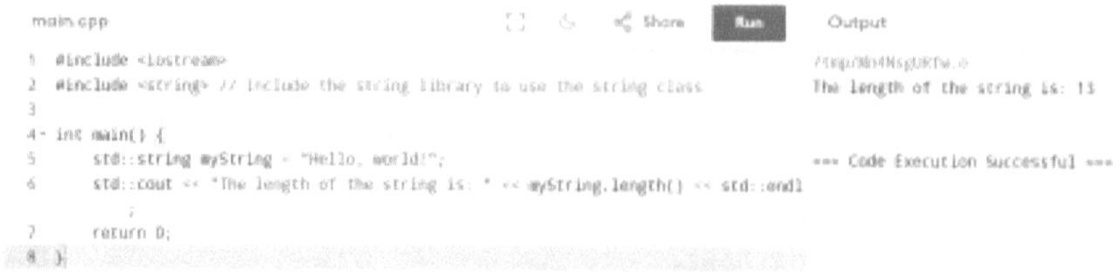

```
main.cpp                                    Share   Run      Output

1  #include <iostream>                                        /tmp/Wb4NsgUKfw.o
2  #include <string> // Include the string library to use     The length of the string is: 13
   the string class
3
4  int main() {                                               === Code Execution Successful ===
5      std::string myString = "Hello, world!";
6      std::cout << "The length of the string is: " << myString.length() << std::endl
7      return 0;
8  }
```

Explanation: In C++, the length() function of the string class is used to obtain the number of characters in a string. This function returns an unsigned integer representing the length of the string. In the example above, myString.length() will return 13, which is the number of characters in the string "Hello, world!" including punctuation and spaces.

The length() function is often used in programs where manipulating text data is necessary, such as parsing inputs, formatting outputs, or simply validating the length of a string against certain criteria. It's an essential function for handling and processing strings in C++.

Access Strings

Here's a coding example in C++ that demonstrates accessing characters within a string:

This is Live Code


```cpp
#include <iostream>
#include <string>
int main() {
std::string str = "Hello, world!";
// Accessing the first character
char firstChar = str[0];
// Accessing the sixth character
char sixthChar = str[5];
std::cout << "First character: " << firstChar << std::endl;
std::cout << "Sixth character: " << sixthChar << std::endl;
return 0;
}
```

- **This is a live coding example**

```
main.cpp                                    Share   Run        Output

 1  #include <iostream>                                /tmp/GhjzwSufgf.o
 2  #include <string>                                  First character: H
 3                                                     Sixth character: ,
 4  int main() {
 5      std::string str = "Hello, world!";
 6                                                     === Code Execution Successful ===
 7      // Accessing the first character
 8      char firstChar = str[0];
 9
10      // Accessing the sixth character
11      char sixthChar = str[5];
12
13      std::cout << "First character: " << firstChar << std::endl;
14      std::cout << "Sixth character: " << sixthChar << std::endl;
15
16      return 0;
17  }
```

Explanation:

Accessing strings in C++ specifically refers to reading or modifying individual characters within a string. In the example above:

- The string str is declared with the value "Hello, world!".
- Characters within a string can be accessed using the square bracket [] notation. Here, str[0] retrieves the first character of the string ('H'), and str[5] retrieves the sixth character (',').
- Each position in the square brackets represents the index of the character in the string, where the index starts from 0. Therefore, str[0] is the first character, str[1] is the second character, and so on.
- This method of accessing strings is useful for iterating over each character, checking or modifying specific characters based on their position.

Special Characters

C++ special characters are symbols that have a specific meaning in the syntax of the language. They're used to perform operations, denote specific constructs, or alter the usual interpretation of sequences of characters. Here's a coding example that uses some of these special characters:

This is live Code


```
#include <iostream>
int main() {
int x = 10;
int y = 20;
int z = x + y; // '+' is a special character used for addition
std::cout << "Result: " << z << std::endl; // ';' ends the statement, '<<' is used for output
return 0;
}
```

- **This is a live coding example**

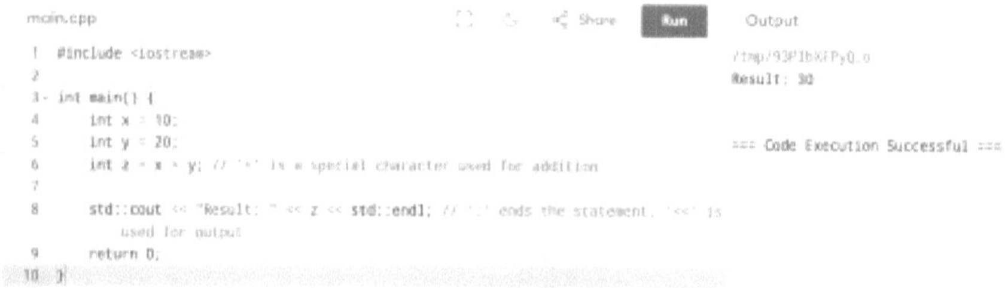

In the example above, several special characters are used:

- # is used to start a preprocessor directive (#include).
- < and > are used to specify include file boundaries.
- { and } denote the beginning and end of a block of code.
- ; marks the end of a statement.
- + is an operator that adds two numbers.
- << is an operator used to send output to the console.
- :: is the scope resolution operator, used here to specify the namespace for cout and endl.

In C++, these special characters are integral to the structure and functionality of the code, influencing how it is parsed and executed by the compiler.

User Input Strings

Here's an example of how to get user input for strings in C++:

This is live Code


```cpp
#include <iostream>
#include <string> // Include the string library
int main() {
std::string name; // Declare a string variable
std::cout << "Enter your name: ";
std::getline(std::cin, name); // Get user input using getline
std::cout << "Hello, " + name + "!"; // Output the input
return 0;
}
```

- **This is a live coding example**

```cpp
main.cpp                                    Share    Run      Output
1  #include <iostream>                                /tmp/KNQKyLkuBa.o
2  #include <string> // Include the string library    Enter your name:
3
4 · int main() {
5      std::string name; // Declare a string variable
6
7      std::cout << "Enter your name: ";
8      std::getline(std::cin, name); // Get user input using getline
9
10     std::cout << "Hello, " + name + "!"; // Output the input
11
12     return 0;
13 }
```

Explanation:

C++ User Input Strings refers to the process of capturing text input from the user in a C++ program, specifically into a string variable. The example above demonstrates this using the getline() function from the <string> library, which allows the entire line of text entered by the user (including spaces) to be stored in a string variable. Here, std::cin is used to capture the input from the standard input (usually the keyboard), and name is the string variable where the input is stored. The getline() function is preferred over cin >> for strings when the input may contain spaces, as cin >> stops reading input at the first whitespace character it encounters.

String Namespace

In C++, the term "namespace" is used to encapsulate identifiers (like variable names, function names, class names) to avoid naming conflicts. When discussing the C++ string, the term "C++ String Namespace" may refer to the namespace in which the string class and its associated functions are defined. The standard string class in C++ is defined within the std namespace and is specifically std::string.

Here's a simple example of using std::string in C++:

This is live Code

Page |

```
#include <iostream>
#include <string>
int main() {
std::string greeting = "Hello, world!";
std::cout << greeting << std::endl;
return 0;
}
```

- **This is a live coding example**

Explanation:

In the code above:

- #include <string> includes the standard library header where the string class is defined.
- std::string greeting = "Hello, world!"; declares a string variable named greeting initialized with "Hello, world!". Here, std::string specifies that we are using the string class from the std namespace.
- std::cout is used to output the string to the console. std::cout is also part of the std namespace, which includes standard input-output library functionalities.

The std namespace is the standard namespace used by C++ Standard Library components. It is designed to contain all the standard classes and functions provided by C++, thus avoiding conflicts with names in user-defined classes or third-party libraries. The use of std:: before string and cout signifies that these entities are being used from the standard namespace, which helps prevent name clashes and clearly indicates where the definitions are coming from.

There isn't a specific "String Namespace" solely for strings; rather, the string class resides within the broader std namespace, along with many other standard library features.

C-Style Strings

Certainly! Let's start with a coding example of C++ C-style strings:

This is live Code

#include <iostream>

int main() {

char greeting[6] = {'H', 'e', 'l', 'l', 'o', '\0'}; // Define a C-style string

std::cout << "Greeting: " << greeting << std::endl; // Output the string

return 0;

}

- **This is a live coding example**

```
main.cpp                              [] ⟳ ⌁ Share  Run    Output

1  #include <iostream>                               /tmp/ilreLXjlrW.o
2                                                    Greeting: Hello
3  int main() {
4      char greeting[6] = {'H', 'e', 'l', 'l', 'o', '\0'};  // Define a C-style
           string                                    === Code Execution Successful ===
5      std::cout << "Greeting: " << greeting << std::endl;  // Output the string
6      return 0;
7  }
```

Explanation of C++ C-Style Strings:

C-style strings in C++ are a way to handle strings borrowed from the C language, represented as arrays of characters terminated by a null character (\0). The null character indicates the end of the string. This method of storing strings directly operates on the raw memory level, which allows for efficient manipulation but also requires careful management to avoid errors such as buffer overflows.

Each character in the array is stored in contiguous memory locations, and the string must be manually managed in terms of memory allocation, reallocation, and deallocation if needed. This style of string handling is different from the std::string class provided by the C++ Standard Library, which handles memory management automatically and provides a richer set of member functions for string manipulation.

Math

C++ Math refers to the mathematical functions and capabilities provided by the C++ Standard Library, particularly through the <cmath> header. This library includes functions for basic mathematical operations, trigonometric calculations, exponential and logarithmic functions, rounding, and other utility operations.

Here's a simple example of C++ code demonstrating some math functions:

This is live Code


```cpp
#include <iostream>
#include <cmath> // Include the cmath library
int main() {
double x = 9.0;
// Square root
std::cout << "Square root of " << x << " is " << sqrt(x) << std::endl;
// Power function
std::cout << x << " raised to the power of 3 is " << pow(x, 3) << std::endl;
// Absolute value
double y = -10.0;
std::cout << "Absolute value of " << y << " is " << fabs(y) << std::endl;
return 0;
}
```

C++ CODING IDEA WITH EXAMPLE

This is a live coding example

```cpp
#include <iostream>
#include <cmath> // Include the cmath library

int main() {
    double x = 9.0;

    // Square root
    std::cout << "Square root of " << x << " is " << sqrt(x) << std::endl;

    // Power function
    std::cout << x << " raised to the power of 3 is " << pow(x, 3) << std::endl;

    // Absolute value
    double y = -10.0;
    std::cout << "Absolute value of " << y << " is " << fabs(y) << std::endl;

    return 0;
}
```

Output

```
Square root of 9 is 3
9 raised to the power of 3 is 729
Absolute value of -10 is 10


=== Code Execution Successful ===
```

In this example:

- sqrt(x) computes the square root of x.
- pow(x, 3) calculates xxx raised to the power of 3.
- fabs(y) returns the absolute value of y.

C++ Math specifically refers to the implementation and use of these mathematical functions that are defined in the <cmath> header. They are highly optimized for performance and are part of the standard library, ensuring portability and reliability across different platforms where C++ code can run.

Booleans

Here's a simple example of using Booleans in C++:

This is live Code

#include <iostream>
using namespace std;
int main() {
bool isCodingFun = true;
bool isFishTasty = false;
cout << "Is coding fun? " << isCodingFun << endl;
cout << "Is fish tasty? " << isFishTasty << endl;
return 0;
}

This is a live coding example

```
main.cpp                              Show   Run      Output

 1  #include <iostream>                      /tmp/DmaVpZyOW6.o
 2  using namespace std;                     Is coding fun? 1
 3                                           Is fish tasty? 0
 4- int main() {
 5      bool isCodingFun = true;
 6      bool isFishTasty = false;            *** Code Execution Successful ***
 7
 8      cout << "Is coding fun? " << isCodingFun << endl;
 9      cout << "Is fish tasty? " << isFishTasty << endl;
10
11      return 0;
12  }
```

"""

In this code, isCodingFun is set to true and isFishTasty is set to false. When we print these values, C++ will output 1 for true and 0 for false.

Explanation of C++ Booleans:

In C++, a Boolean is a data type that can hold one of two values: true or false. It's used to perform logical operations, often in flow control (like if statements and loops) where decisions need to be made based on the truth value of expressions. The Boolean data type in C++ is denoted by the keyword bool. When used in conditions, true is equivalent to any nonzero value, and false is equivalent to zero. This data type is integral to decision-making processes in programming where binary choices are involved.

Boolean Expressions

Here's an example of a C++ Boolean expression:
This is live Code


```cpp
#include <iostream>

using namespace std;

int main() {

int a = 10;

int b = 20;

bool result = (a < b); // Boolean expression

cout << "The result of the Boolean expression (a < b) is: " << result << endl;

return 0;

}
```

This is a live coding example

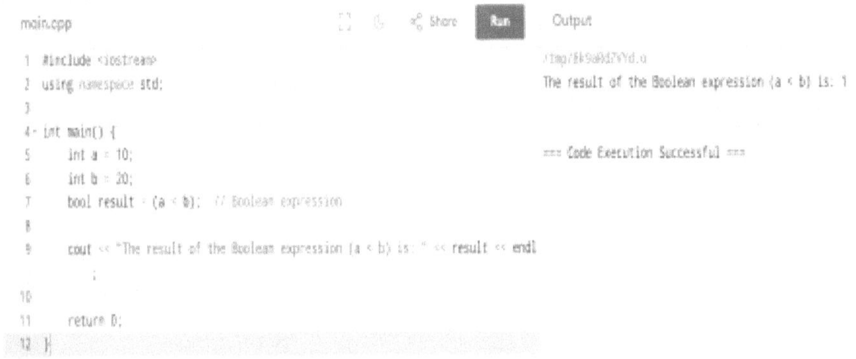

```
main.cpp                          Share   Run      Output

1  #include <iostream>                    /tmp/8k9aNd7xYd.o
2  using namespace std;                   The result of the Boolean expression (a < b) is: 1
3
4- int main() {
5      int a = 10;                        === Code Execution Successful ===
6      int b = 20;
7      bool result = (a < b);  // Boolean expression
8
9      cout << "The result of the Boolean expression (a < b) is: " << result << endl
10
11     return 0;
12 }
```

In this code, (a < b) is a Boolean expression that compares the values of a and b. The expression evaluates to true because a is indeed less than b, and true in C++ is represented as 1 when outputted.

Explanation of C++ Boolean Expressions

In C++, a Boolean expression is any expression that can be evaluated to return a value of true or false. These expressions are commonly used for making decisions within the code, particularly in control flow statements like if, while, and for. Boolean expressions use relational operators such as < (less than), > (greater than), == (equal to), != (not equal to), <= (less than or equal to), and >= (greater than or equal to), as well as logical operators like && (logical AND), || (logical OR), and ! (logical NOT).

The result of a Boolean expression is a bool data type, which is a built-in type in C++ that takes the values true or false. These expressions are fundamental for controlling program flow and making logical decisions based on the conditions evaluated.

If ... Else

Here's a coding example using C++ if ... else statements:

This is live Code


```cpp
#include <iostream>
using namespace std;
int main() {
int number;
cout << "Enter an integer: ";
cin >> number;
if (number % 2 == 0) {
cout << number << " is even.";
} else {
cout << number << " is odd.";
}
return 0;
}
```

This is a live coding example

In C++, if ... else statements are used to execute different blocks of code based on a condition. Here's what each part does:

- **if statement**: It evaluates the condition inside the parentheses (). If the condition is true, the code block following the if statement is executed.
- **Condition**: In this example, number % 2 == 0 checks whether the number is even by using the modulus operator % which gives the remainder of the division of number by 2. If the remainder is 0, the condition is true, meaning the number is even.
- **else statement**: This is executed if the condition in the if statement is false. In this case, if the number is not even (i.e., it's odd), the code block following the else statement is executed.

Using if ... else allows a program to choose between two paths of execution based on the truth value of a condition.

Else

In C++, the else statement is used in conjunction with if statements to execute a block of code when the condition specified in the if part is not met. Here's a simple example to illustrate how else is used:

This is live Code


```cpp
#include <iostream>
using namespace std;
int main() {
int number = 10;
if (number > 10) {
cout << "The number is greater than 10." << endl;
} else {
cout << "The number is not greater than 10." << endl;
}
return 0;
}
```

This is a live coding example

Explanation:

- if (number > 10) checks whether the number is greater than 10.
- If this condition is true, it executes the code inside the if block, which would print "The number is greater than 10."
- If the condition is false, as it is in this example since number equals 10, it executes the code inside the else block, which prints "The number is not greater than 10."

The else keyword provides a way to execute a different set of instructions when the if condition fails. This is useful for handling various scenarios and outcomes in a program.

Else If

Here's a coding example using else if in C++:


```cpp
This is live Code
#include <iostream>
using namespace std;
int main() {
int number = 15;
if (number > 20) {
cout << "Number is greater than 20." << endl;
} else if (number > 10) {
cout << "Number is greater than 10 but not greater than 20." << endl;
} else {
cout << "Number is 10 or less." << endl;
}
return 0;
}
```

This is a live coding example

```
main.cpp                              Share    Run      Output

 1  #include <iostream>                          /tmp/PjALxGiqj.h x
 2  using namespace std;                         Number is greater than 10 but not greater than 20.
 3
 4  int main() {
 5      int number = 15;                         *** Code Execution Successful ***
 6
 7      if (number > 20) {
 8          cout << "Number is greater than 20." << endl;
 9      } else if (number > 10) {
10          cout << "Number is greater than 10 but not greater than 20." << endl;
11      } else {
12          cout << "Number is 10 or less." << endl;
13      }
14
15      return 0;
16  }
```

In this example, the else if statement is used to create a chain of conditions. Here's what else if specifically means in C++:

else if: This is used when you want to test multiple conditions in sequence. If the initial if condition is false, then the program checks the condition in the else if block. You can have multiple else if blocks following an if, each checking different conditions.

The else if allows for more specific checks and responses based on different criteria. Only if the previous if or else if conditions are false, will the else if condition be evaluated.

If an else if condition is true, its associated block of code runs, and the rest of the else if blocks (if any) along with the else block are skipped.

In summary, else if provides a way to handle multiple, distinct conditions efficiently, allowing different blocks of code to execute based on which condition is true first.

Short Hand If Else

The shorthand if-else in C++, also known as the ternary operator, is a condensed way to express simple decision-making in code. Here's an example of its use:

This is live Code


```cpp
#include <iostream>
using namespace std;
int main() {
int x = 20;
int y = 15;
string result = (x > y) ? "x is greater than y" : "x is not greater than y";
cout << result;
return 0;
}
```

```
main.cpp                                    Share    Run      Output

1  #include <iostream>                                        /tmp/askEKks02r.o
2  using namespace std;                                       x is greater than y
3
4· int main() {                                               === Code Execution Successful ===
5      int x = 20;
6      int y = 15;
7      string result = (x > y) ? "x is greater than y" : "x is not greater than y";
8      cout << result;
9      return 0;
10 }
```

This is a live coding example

In this example, the ternary operator ?: checks the condition (x > y). If this condition is true, it assigns the string "x is greater than y" to the variable result. If the condition is false, it assigns "x is not greater than y" instead.

The general syntax of the ternary operator is:

condition ? expression_if_true : expression_if_false;

It's a quick way to write an if-else statement when each branch of the condition executes a single statement. This helps in making the code more compact and easy to read when dealing with simple conditions.

Conclusion

As we draw the curtain on "C++ Coding Idea with Example: Learn C++ Efficiently and Dominate the Programming World," it's important to reflect on the journey we've embarked upon together. This book, crafted meticulously by Billy H. Green, was designed to teach you the syntax of C++ and empower you with the skills needed to apply these concepts in the real world. By now, you should feel a newfound confidence in your ability to navigate the landscape of C++ programming, equipped with the knowledge and practical examples provided throughout the pages. Throughout this guide, we've explored the fundamentals and more complex aspects of C++, each chapter building upon the last to form a comprehensive understanding. The examples and real-world applications discussed have illustrated C++'s capabilities and prepared you to apply these concepts in various scenarios, be it in software development, game programming, or systems engineering.

Now, as you move forward, remember that mastery of any programming language, including C++, is not achieved overnight but through continuous practice and learning. Please revisit the concepts discussed, experiment with the code, and challenge yourself with new projects that push your learning boundaries. Your journey does not end here. The programming world is dynamic and ever-evolving, and your continued education and adaptability will be critical to your success. Whether you dive deeper into C++, explore other programming languages, or start applying your skills in professional settings, you are now better equipped to face those challenges. Thank you for choosing this book as your guide to C++ programming. May the ideas and examples you've learned here inspire and guide you as you forge your path in the programming world. Remember, every coder was once a beginner, and every expert coder never stopped learning. Keep coding, keep creating, and dominate the programming world.

The End

Page |

Also by Billy H. Green

C++ Coding Idea with Example